Great
Re

Collected by Lynn Hattery-Beyer

Editors: Miriam Canter, Dorothy Crum,
Cheryl Ferguson, Joan Liffring-Zug
and Michelle Nagle Spencer

Cover Calligraphy by Esther Feske
German Folk Designs by Helen Blanck

ISBN 0-941016-49-8

PENFIELD PRESS
215 BROWN STREET
IOWA CITY, IA 52245-5842

Contents

About the Author.......... 4
German Folk Art Designs.......... 5
German-American Sites.......... 6
Familiar German Words.......... 7
German Table Blessings.......... 8
German Traditions.......... 11
German Menu Suggestions.......... 14
Beverages.......... 15
Salads.......... 22
Soups.......... 40
Breads.......... 53
Main Course Dishes.......... 69
Vegetables.......... 98
Cakes and Desserts.......... 119

About the Author

Lynn Hattery-Beyer of Iowa went to West Germany to study, and stayed. She lives with her husband and two small children in the village of Wolfegg in southern Germany, north of Lake Constance. Lynn and Lothar Beyer use wood-burning stoves in their historic farm house. She works as a translator and English tutor.

While visiting her parents, Don and Mary Lou Hattery of Cedar Rapids, Iowa for several months, Lynn compiled this book of *Great German Recipes*. Another purpose of her visit was to enroll her children in kindergarten and preschool in America so they would learn to speak English better (as a second language).

In 1970-71, the Hatterys hosted a German foreign exchange student. In return, Lynn visited the student's family and ultimately she enrolled at the University of Bielefeld in West Germany, where she received a master's degree in education.

German Folk Art Designs

Artist Helen Blanck of Minneapolis, Minnesota, has created the Bauernmalerei border for the front cover of this book and inside designs typical of this style of folk art.

According to Helen, "this art predates the Norwegian rosemaling by 200 to 300 years." Different provinces of Germany produced various styles. In the 1500s heraldic and geometric designs were used. Later floral designs were combined with the earlier styles, adding birds and people. Scrolls became a framing device. The rose and tulip were favorites and soon the German love of flowers included daisies, poppies, delphiniums, violets, pomegranate fruit, morning glories and others. Baby's breath, leaves and buds were used to fill in areas.

German-American Sites

Many Americans can trace their ancestry to German-speaking immigrants. Germans were one of the largest immigrant groups. German-speaking troops fought on both sides of the American Revolution and the Civil War. Other Germans came to America seeking freedom from military service and the right to worship as they pleased. Their peace-loving descendants include the Mennonites, Brethren, and Amish who live in Pennsylvania, Ohio, Indiana, Illinois, Iowa, Minnesota, Kansas and elsewhere. These people are noted for their Pennsylvania Dutch (German-American) cooking. A famous restaurant is Miller's Smorgasbord at Ronks, Pennsylvania. German-speaking immigrants who went to Wisconsin, Texas and other states were seeking freedom and opportunity. Many were from Switzerland and the German-speaking areas of the old Austro-Hungarian Empire.

Familiar German Words

Willkommen—Welcome, we want you.
Auf Wiedersehen—Until we meet again.
Gemütlichkeit (pronounced ge-MEWT-lech-kite)—A little hard to define in English, it means a feeling of warmth, friendship, hospitality and coziness. You'll find it in literature from German-American sites such as the Amana Colonies in Iowa. Their family-style restaurants feature *Gemütlichkeit,* as do the "Pennslvania Dutch" in Lancaster County.
Bratwurst—A German sausage. One usually thinks of brats and beer.
Sauerbraten—Beef or pork marinated in vinegar before cooking.
Wiener Schnitzel—"Vienna cutlet" of breaded veal.
Kuchen—A general term for cake.
Oktoberfest—A fall beer party.
Maifest—A "Welcome to Spring" festival.

German Table Blessings

Komm Herr Jesu, sei unser Gast, und segne was Du uns bescheret hast.
(In unison): Amen. Gott segne uns.

Come Lord Jesus, be our Guest and let this food to us be blessed.
(In unison): Amen. God bless us.

This is a table grace commonly said by families in the Amana Colonies in Iowa. It is prayed just as frequently in German as in English before beginning a meal. One person says the prayer and everyone joins in for the final blessing.

German Table Blessings

Enable us to use Thy manifold blessings
with moderation;
Grant our hearts wisdom to avoid excess
in eating and drinking
and in the cares of this life;
Teach us to put our trust in Thee
and to await Thy helping hand.

—Traditional Amish Prayer

German Table Blessings

Jedes Tierlein hat sein Fressen,
Jede Blume trinkt von Dir,
Lass auch uns Dich nicht vergessen,
Lieber Gott wir danken Dir.

Every animal is given food,
Each flower gets a drink,
Don't let us forget Thee either,
Dear Lord, we thank Thee.

—German Children's Blessing

Notes on German Traditions

German eating habits differ from ours in many respects.

Unless drinking wine or beer, Germans rarely include beverages in their meals. Beer is often served at supper, especially when the meal consists of sauerkraut and sausages or smoked pork. Wine is an important part of any formal meal. Milk is a beverage unknown to most German adults. Juice is served to children and to those preferring non-alcoholic beverages at parties. No German in his or her right mind would ever drink water straight from the tap, although they do often drink carbonated mineral water.

If a meal is to consist of more than one course, the first course is rarely an appetizer as we know it. Germans would begin with a light soup, such as **Liver Dumplings**

continued

German Traditions *continued*

In Broth or **Yarn Soup**. The main course would include: meat or fish; either potatoes, noodles or rice; a vegetable and a salad. If dessert is served, it is very light, either fresh fruit, as in **Raspberry Snow** or a pudding, such as **Bavarian Cream.** More likely than not, an after-dinner liqueur would take the place of a dessert.

All of the luscious pastry and cakes are served at "Kaffee", or coffee time, in the middle of the afternoon. Most German households celebrate this daily ritual of gathering together for coffee and cake sometime between 3 and 4 o'clock in the afternoon. Although rather simple on weekdays, the cakes served on weekends, such as **Frankfurt Tube Cake** or **Blackberry Cake,** are often testimonies of the housewife's talents.

continued

German Traditions *continued*

Baked goods are not restricted to cakes. The most important part of a German breakfast or supper is bread. Breakfast usually consists of bread with cheese, bread with cold cuts and bread with homemade jam. Supper is more of the same, substituting tomato slices and pickles for the jam. Since it plays such an important role, there are usually several sorts of bread to choose from, and they are always fresh.

All in all, fewer prepared foods are used in a German kitchen. Few recipes call for canned soup, prepared mayonnaise or cake mixes. Instead, they give instructions for making things from scratch. Fresh ingredients are also preferred over frozen or canned food. If a German cook cannot obtain the fresh fruits, vegetables or meats called for in a recipe, she would save this recipe for the season when the ingredients are available.

German Menu Suggestions

Light Meals:

Lentil Stew (pg. 43)
Heidelberg Rye Bread (pg. 54)
Tomato Salad (pg. 24)

Herring in Sour Cream (pg. 97)
Boiled Potatoes (pg. 111)
Bean Salad (pg. 36)

Blind Chicken Soup (pg. 46)
Pumpernickel (pg. 58)

Apple Streusel Pie (pg. 143)

Full Course Meals:

Broth with Pancake Strips (pg. 51)
Braised Rabbit (pg. 85)
Potato Dumplings (pg. 116)
Red Cabbage (pg. 100)
Bavarian Cream (pg. 147)

Sauerbraten (pg. 70)
Swabian Noodles (pg. 72)
Baby Peas and Carrots (pg. 99)
Elisabeth's Strawberries (pg. 150)

Beverages

To good eating belongs good drinking.

Auf einen guten Bissen gehört ein guter Trunk.

Fruit Punch — Bowle

6 ripe, peeled peaches
  or 8 unpeeled apricots
  or 1 sliced pineapple
  or 1 qt. strawberries

1/2 cup powdered sugar
1 cup dry sherry
4 bottles dry white wine

Slice one of the above fruits and place in a large bowl. Sprinkle with powdered sugar. Pour sherry over fruit, cover and let stand for at least 4 hours. Add wine and stir. Serve cold.

Berlin Punch

Berliner Bowle

2 bottles ginger ale
1 bottle champagne
2 Tbsp. sugar
half a lemon

Store ginger ale and champagne in refrigerator. When well-chilled pour into punch bowl. Press lemon and dissolve sugar in lemon juice. Add to punch bowl. Float lemon rind in punch for half an hour. Remove before serving. Serve well-chilled.

May Wine — Maiwein

- 10 sprigs young waldmeister or sweet woodruff
- 1 cup powdered sugar
- 1 bottle Moselle or other dry white wine
- 1/2 cup brandy
- 3 bottles Moselle wine
- 1 qt. carbonated water or champagne

Combine first four ingredients in a bowl. Cover and allow to stand for no longer than 30 minutes. Remove the waldmeister. Stir thoroughly and pour into a punch bowl. Add remaining ingredients and stir. Float sprigs of waldmeister in punch bowl and serve chilled.

Rhine Wine Cup

Rheinweinbowle

1/2 cup water
1 cup sugar
1 1/2 cups lemon juice
1/2 cup brandy
1 1/2 cups dry sherry
3 bottles dry white Rhine wine
1 qt. carbonated water

Combine water and sugar in saucepan. Boil for 5 minutes. Chill. Mix all ingredients together in a chilled punch bowl. Add ice and serve.

Mulled Wine — Glühwein

1 liter red wine
1/4 cup sugar
1 Tbsp. lemon juice
4 whole cloves
2 cinnamon sticks
1 tangerine, divided into slices

Heat wine, sugar, lemon juice and spices for 10 minutes over low heat. Do not allow wine to boil! Remove whole spices and serve in mugs or heatproof glasses. Float 1 or 2 tangerine slices in each glass.

Coffee and love are best when they're hot.

Kaffee und die Liebe schmecken am besten wenn sie heiss sind.

Salads

A hungry stomach has no ears.

Ein hungriger Magen hat keine Ohren.

Dandelion Salad — Löwenzahnsalat

1 lb. young dandelions
1/8 lb. bacon, diced
3 onions, finely chopped
1 Tbsp. vinegar
1/2 tsp. salt
1 Tbsp. sugar
1 Tbsp. water
2 tsp. finely chopped fresh herbs

Remove blossoms from dandelions. Cut stem and youngest leaves into small pieces and wash. Fry bacon and onions. Place in salad bowl together with dandelion leaves. Combine vinegar, salt, sugar, water and herbs to make a salad dressing. Pour over salad and toss just before serving.

Tomato Salad — Tomatensalat

1 cup water
1 Tbsp. vinegar
1 tsp. salt
1 large onion
3 medium-sized tomatoes
2 salt herring, boned
4 Tbsp. chopped parsley
1/2 cup mayonnaise

Combine water, vinegar and salt in a saucepan and bring to a boil. Peel and thinly slice onion. Add to boiling water and cook until glassy. Remove from heat, drain and cool. Thinly slice tomatoes. Cut herring into bite-sized pieces. In a glass salad bowl alternately layer onion, tomatoes, herring and parsley. Pour mayonnaise over top layer and chill until ready to serve.

Sauerkraut Salad — Krautsalat

1 lb. can sauerkraut, drained
3 Tbsp. salad oil
2 - 3 onions, finely chopped
2 Tbsp. caraway seeds
2 apples, grated

Put sauerkraut into a salad bowl and loosen it with a fork. Heat oil in a saucepan and pour over sauerkraut. Add onions, caraway seeds and grated apples. Mix well.

Grated Beets — Rote Bete

3 medium-sized beets, uncooked
1 sour apple, grated
3 Tbsp. salad oil
1 1/2 Tbsp. lemon juice
1/2 tsp. salt
2 Tbsp. light cream
1 small onion, finely chopped
1 Tbsp. finely chopped parsley

Scrub beets thoroughly under running water. Peel and grate beets finely. Combine with apple in a medium-sized salad bowl. Beat oil, lemon juice and salt with a fork until thick. Stir in cream, chopped onion and parsley. Pour over salad and toss well.

Cucumbers — Gurkensalat

5 large cucumbers
2 Tbsp. salt
2 cups sour cream
1/4 cup wine vinegar
1 tsp. freshly ground black pepper
2 tsp. minced chives

Wash, trim and peel cucumbers completely. Slice them thinly and place in a salad bowl. Sprinkle with salt and let stand 30 minutes. Drain off liquid. Add other ingredients and mix well. Cover and chill for at least 1 hour (the longer they sit the better they are).

Baldwin Heritage Museum Association, Elberta, Alabama

Pickled Cabbage — Rotkohlsalat

1 head red cabbage	2 cups water
salt	2 cups sugar
2 cups vinegar	

Shred red cabbage, sprinkle with a little salt and place in a bowl. Combine vinegar, water and sugar in a saucepan and bring to a boil. Pour hot liquid over cabbage and refrigerate for at least 24 hours. Will keep in refrigerator for at least 2 weeks.

Ronneburg Restaurant, Amana, Iowa

German Coleslaw — Kohlsalat

1 medium-sized head white cabbage
2 slices bacon, diced
1/2 cup water
3 Tbsp. salad oil
1 1/2 Tbsp. vinegar
1/2 tsp. salt
1 tsp. finely chopped parsley

Remove coarse outer leaves from cabbage and cut head into quarters. Remove the core. Shred cabbage finely and wash thoroughly. Fry bacon in a large pot. Add shredded cabbage and continue to cook for 5 minutes, stirring constantly. Add water and simmer until cabbage is just tender. Combine salad oil, vinegar, salt and parsley and pour over warm cabbage. Cool before serving.

Warm Potato Salad — Kartoffelsalat

1 3/4 lb. potatoes
1/2 cup stock or water
1 onion, finely chopped
4 slices bacon, diced and fried
salt and pepper
vinegar
3 Tbsp. finely chopped chives

Cook scrubbed potatoes in boiling water until done. Remove from heat, douse with cold water and peel while still hot. Slice potatoes immediately and put them in a bowl with warm stock or water. Add onion and fried bacon. Season to taste with salt and pepper, vinegar and chives. Serve warm.

Macaroni Salad — Nudelsalat

- 2 cups uncooked macaroni
- 4 dill pickles, diced
- 1 cup cooked peas
- 3/4 cup mayonnaise
- 2 hard-cooked eggs, quartered
- 1 tomato, quartered

Cook macaroni, rinse and drain. Combine macaroni, pickles, peas and mayonnaise in a salad bowl and mix carefully. Garnish with eggs and tomato.

Waldorf Salad

1/2 lb. potatoes
1 cup sliced celery
1 1/2 cups diced apple
2 pickles, diced
1 Tbsp. chopped nuts

3 Tbsp. salad oil
2 Tbsp. lemon juice
1/2 tsp. salt
1 tsp. finely chopped parsley

Scrub and boil potatoes until done. Douse with cold water, peel and cut them into bite-sized pieces. Combine potatoes, celery, apple, pickles and nuts in a large bowl. Beat oil, lemon juice and salt with a fork until thick and creamy. Stir in parsley; pour over salad and toss. Let stand 2-3 hours before serving.

Pickled Pigs Feet

4 pigs feet
water, salted
2 cups vinegar
2 Tbsp. salt
1 Tbsp. whole cloves
1/2 tsp. black pepper
1 small stick cinnamon
1 cup chopped dill pickles

Scrape and clean pigs feet well. Put in a kettle to boil with enough salt water to cover. Simmer for 4 hours or until meat will separate easily from bones. Remove feet and add vinegar, salt, pepper and spices to stock in which meat was cooked. Boil for 30 minutes. Strain liquid and remove spices. Pick meat off feet. Place pieces of meat and chopped pickles in a glass loaf pan and pour stock over it. Chill until completely cold. Slice and serve. May be made ahead of time and kept in refrigerator.

Crab Salad — Krabbensalat

9 oz. crab meat
(fresh, canned or frozen)
juice of 1 lemon
salt and pepper
dash of paprika

1 tsp. sugar
1 onion, finely chopped
2 Tbsp. oil
1 Tbsp. chopped parsley

Flake crab meat with a fork and sprinkle it with lemon juice. Season to taste with salt, pepper, paprika and sugar. Stir in onion and oil. Sprinkle with parsley. Good served with toast and butter.

Bremen Herring Salad

Marinade:
2 Tbsp. milk
4 Tbsp. lemon juice
4 Tbsp. salad oil
2 Tbsp. mild mustard
4 Tbsp. finely chopped onion
4 Tbsp. cranberry sauce
1 Tbsp. capers
salt and pepper

4 salted herring, boned
3/4 lb. roast veal, cubed
3 apples, diced
5 hard-cooked eggs

Combine ingredients for marinade in a medium-sized bowl. Cut herring into small pieces and add to marinade, together with veal, pickles and apples. Slice 4 eggs in half, remove yolks and dice the egg whites. Add egg whites to salad and toss carefully. Garnish with parsley and slices of remaining egg.

Bean Salad — Bohnensalat

1 lb. fresh green string beans
water, salted
1/2 - 1 cup chopped onion
4 Tbsp. bacon grease
4 Tbsp. vinegar
3 Tbsp. sugar
1 - 2 tsp. salt
dash of pepper

Wash, break stem ends and pull off any strings from beans. Cut them lengthwise or diagonally. Cover with salted water and cook until tender, but not soft, about 15 minutes. Drain. Fry onion in bacon grease over very low heat until glassy, about 5 minutes. Add beans and remaining ingredients. Mix well and heat thoroughly to improve flavor. Serve slightly warm.

Hermann Cook Book, Hermann, Missouri

Sweet Dill Pickles — Eingemachte Gurken

cucumbers
several cloves of garlic
fresh dill
2 cups vinegar
2 cups water
3 cups sugar
2 Tbs. salt

Slice cucumbers thin and place in sterile jars. Place a garlic clove and some dill in each jar. Heat vinegar, water, sugar and salt in saucepan. Pour over cucumbers. Process for 5 minutes after they begin to boil.

Beet Relish

1 qt. beets, boiled and shredded
medium fine
1 qt. raw cabbage, shredded fine
2 cups sugar

1 Tbsp. salt
1 tsp. pepper
1/2 cup grated horseradish
cider vinegar

Mix all ingredients with a little cider vinegar. Pack in sterile jars and add more vinegar to cover. Seal cold. Will keep refrigerated for months.

Sour Cream Salad — Sauerrahmsalat

1 head lettuce
1 small onion, finely chopped
1/2 tsp. salt
dash of pepper
3 Tbsp. vinegar
1/2 cup sour cream

Wash and shred lettuce. Mix onion, salt, pepper, vinegar and sour cream. Pour over lettuce and toss.

Ox Yoke Inn, Amana, Iowa

Soups

Many cooks spoil the broth.

Viele Köche verderben den Brei.

Liver Dumplings in Broth
Bayerische Leberknödelsuppe

5 pieces dry bread
1/2 cup hot milk
1 lb. liver
1 onion, finely chopped
5 Tbsp. butter
2 eggs
1/2 cup bread crumbs
salt and pepper
1 tsp. dried marjoram
1 tsp. finely chopped parsley
1/2 tsp. garlic powder
1 qt. stock
1 Tbsp. chopped chives

Soak bread in milk. Squeeze out excess moisture and mince together with liver. Fry onion in butter and add to liver mixture. Stir in eggs, bread crumbs, spices and herbs. Shape into spoon-sized dumplings and cook in salted boiling water. Heat stock separately. When dumplings rise to surface remove and add to hot stock. Sprinkle with chives and serve very hot.

Onion Soup — Rheinische Zwiebelsuppe

2 qts. water, salted
2 lbs. small onions, peeled
2 1/2 lbs. potatoes, peeled
salt and pepper
3/4 lb. smoked sausage, diced
1/8 lb. bacon, diced and fried
4 Tbsp. butter

Bring water to a boil in large stockpot. Add peeled onions and cook until tender. Boil potatoes separately and purée. Add to onions, stirring until well-mixed. Cook over low heat until thickened. Season with salt and pepper. Add sausage, bacon and butter. Serve with white bread.

Lentil Stew — Linseneintopf

2 1/4 cups lentils
1/2 cup diced bacon
3 onions, chopped
2 Tbsp. vinegar
1 tsp. salt
1 Tbsp. sugar
1 tsp. pepper
pinch of thyme
1 bay leaf
1 cup red wine
2 medium-sized potatoes, diced
1 cup water

Soak lentils overnight. Pour off excess liquid. Fry bacon and onions. Combine with lentils in large stockpot. Add remaining ingredients, stirring well. Cook over low heat for 1 1/2 - 2 hours. Serve with dark rye bread and wieners.

Cabbage and Almond Soup

1 large head of cabbage, shredded in 1/4 inch pieces
1 large onion, julienned to 1/4 inch
6 qts. chicken stock
1/2- 2/3 cup sliced, blanched almonds
salt and pepper
1/2 cup honey
1/4 cup vinegar
fresh watercress to garnish

Place first four ingredients into large stockpot. Bring contents to a full, rolling boil. Reduce heat, cover and simmer until cabbage is tender. Season with salt and pepper. Add honey or vinegar, as needed. Garnish each bowl with a sprig of fresh watercress. Makes 20 servings.

Historic Strasburg Inn, Strasburg, Pennsylvania

Hearty Barley Soup

2 cups water
1/2 cup dry beans
8 cups stock or beef bouillon
1 carrot, sliced
1 onion, chopped
1 stalk celery, sliced
1/2 cup cooked lentils
1/2 cup barley
1 8-oz. can tomato soup (optional)
1/2 cup rolled oats, quick or regular
1/2 cup frozen green peas
parsley, salt and pepper to taste

Put water and beans in a saucepan. Bring to a boil, shut off heat and let cool for 1 hour. Drain. Combine all ingredients in a stockpot and simmer for 2 hours.

Blind Chicken Soup — Blindhuhn

3 qts. water
2 1/2 cups dried kidney beans
1/2 lb. bacon, unsliced
1 ham bone
2 1/2 cups green beans, cut in pieces
1 cup sliced carrots
1 lb. potatoes, peeled and diced
1 1/2 cups sliced apple
2 onions, sliced
3 Tbsp. bacon grease
salt and pepper
1 Tbsp. chopped parsley

Soak kidney beans overnight. Add bacon and ham to beans and water in which they have soaked and cook for 45 minutes. Add green beans, carrots and potatoes. Cook for another 30 minutes. Remove ham bone and bacon. Add apple slices. Fry onions in bacon grease until golden brown and add to vegetables. Season with salt and pepper and sprinkle with parsley. Slice bacon and serve on top of soup.

Heaven and Earth — Himmel und Erde

1 1/3 cups water
1/2 tsp. salt
3 1/2 lbs. potatoes, peeled and diced
3 apples, peeled and quartered
1 tsp. salt
1 Tbsp. sugar
1 Tbsp. vinegar
1/4 lb. bacon, diced
2 onions, sliced

Bring water and salt to boil in stockpot. Add potatoes and boil until tender. Add apples, return to boil and cook until tender. Season with salt, sugar and vinegar. Fry bacon and onion slices until brown. Pour over potatoes and apples and serve.

Bread Soup — Brotsuppe

1/2 lb. dry bread
1 qt. water or milk
1/2 tsp. anise seeds
1/2 tsp. fennel seeds
1/2 tsp. salt
1 tsp. sugar
1/2 tsp. vanilla extract

Break bread into small pieces and soak in water or milk for several hours. Add anise and fennel seeds, bring to a boil and simmer until bread is soft. Purée or rub through a sieve and season with salt, sugar and vanilla.

Fresh Fruit Soup — Obstschale

1 lb. fresh fruit (apples, pears, cherries, plums, gooseberries or rhubarb)
1 qt. cold water
1 twist of lemon peel
2 Tbsp. cornstarch
2 Tbsp. cold water
1 tsp. cinnamon
1/4 - 1/2 cup sugar
1 Tbsp. lemon juice or dry wine

Wash and slice any combination of fruits listed above. Place in a saucepan, cover with cold water, add lemon peel and simmer until tender. Purée fruit or rub through a sieve, leaving a few pieces as garnish. Bring the fruit purée to a boil and remove from heat. Mix cornstarch and 2 Tbsp. water and stir into hot purée. Return to heat and bring to a boil, stirring constantly until thickened. Season with cinnamon, sugar and lemon juice or wine. Serve hot or cold.

Yarn Soup — Baumwollsuppe

5 cups strong broth
2 eggs
2 tsp. flour
1/4 cup light cream
2 tsp. butter
pinch of nutmeg

Simmer broth in large saucepan. Combine remaining ingredients in a small bowl, stirring with a fork until well-blended. Hold bowl 6 inches above saucepan. While stirring broth with a fork in one hand, slowly pour a stream of beaten egg mixture into simmering broth. Catch egg with fork as it hits the broth and pull it into long threads. Repeat 2 or 3 times until egg mixture is gone. Simmer for 1 minute and serve at once.

Pancake Strips — Flädele

2/3 cup flour
1/2 tsp. salt
1 egg
1/2 cup water
1 tsp. chopped parsley
1 Tbsp. butter

Combine flour, salt, egg and water in a mixing bowl. Batter should not be lumpy. Add parsley. Melt butter in frying pan, pour in just enough batter to coat bottom of pan and fry on both sides until golden brown. Cool. Roll pancakes and cut into thin strips. Add to any clear soup or broth.

Liver Dumplings — Leberklösschen

1 lb. liver, ground
2 cups bread crumbs
1 egg
1 cup flour
salt and pepper to taste
1 onion, minced

Mix liver, bread crumbs, egg, flour, salt, pepper and onion. Drop 1 teaspoon of mixture at a time into boiling salted water. Boil for 15 minutes, and remove dumplings. Add to any warm broth.

Colony Inn, Amana, Iowa

Breads

It's better to have your own bread than someone else's roast.

Besser eigenes Brot als fremder Braten.

Heidelberg Rye Bread — Roggenbrot

3 cups bread flour
3 cups rye flour
2 pkgs. dry yeast
3/8 cup cocoa
1 1/2 Tbsp. sugar
1 Tbsp. salt
1 1/2 Tbsp. caraway seeds
2 cups hot water (120°-130°)
1/3 cup molasses
2 Tbsp. shortening

In large mixing bowl combine 1 1/2 cups bread flour, 1 1/2 cups rye flour, yeast, cocoa, sugar, salt and caraway seeds. Add water, molasses and shortening. Beat at high speed for 3 minutes. Gradually add remaining bread and rye flour until dough is no longer sticky. Knead for 5 minutes. Cover. Let rise for 20 minutes.

continued

Heidelberg Rye Bread *continued*

Punch down and divide dough in half. Shape into round balls and flatten slightly. Place on greased baking sheet, brush with oil and cover loosely with plastic wrap. Refrigerate for 2 - 24 hours. Allow loaves to stand at room temperature while oven preheats to 400°. Slash an X on top of each loaf and bake 30-40 minutes.

Lynn says: "The bread recipes in this book will also work when all-purpose flour is used. Because of its higher gluten content, however, bread flour will make the bread rise better."

Old Order Amish Bread

1 pkg. dry yeast
1/2 cup lukewarm water
1 3/4 cups hot water
1/3 cup sugar
1 1/2 tsp. salt
1/2 cup oil
7 - 8 cups bread flour

Dissolve yeast in lukewarm water and set aside. Blend hot water, sugar, salt, oil and 2 cups flour in a mixing bowl. Add yeast and 2 more cups of flour. Beat 2 minutes at medium speed. Knead 10 minutes, adding remaining flour until dough is no longer sticky. Cover and let rise until double in volume. Punch down and let rise again. Punch down and form into 3 equal loaves. Place loaves in greased 8 1/2 x 4 1/2-inch loaf pans. Cover and let rise until 1 inch above edge of pans (about 45 minutes). Preheat oven to 400° and bake for 10 minutes. Reduce heat to 350° and continue baking for 30 minutes more. Remove from pans immediately and cool on racks.

Vienna Bread

3 Tbsp. dry yeast
2 Tbsp. sugar
5 cups warm water, divided
1/2 cup wheat germ
4 Tbsp. sugar or honey
4 Tbsp. shortening
3 tsp. salt
10 cups all-purpose flour
2 cups whole wheat flour

Dissolve yeast and 2 Tbsp. sugar in 1/2 cup warm water. Set aside until foamy. In a large mixing bowl combine 4 1/2 cups warm water, wheat germ, sugar or honey, shortening and salt. Add yeast mixture and stir thoroughly. Add flours and knead for 10 minutes. Let dough rise for 15 minutes, punch down. Repeat 3 times, then shape dough into 4 loaves. Place each in a greased 9x 5-inch loaf pan. Bake at 375° for 40 minutes or until bread sounds hollow when knocked.

The Kalona Heritage, Amish and Mennonite Culture (Iowa)

Pumpernickel

2 pkgs. dry yeast
1 1/4 cups warm water
2 tsp. salt
1/3 cup molasses
1 Tbsp. caraway seeds
1 Tbsp. shortening

2 cups rye flour
2 - 2 1/4 cups white flour
2 tsp. corn meal
1 egg white
3/4 tsp. caraway seeds

In large bowl dissolve yeast in warm water. Stir in salt, molasses, 1 Tbsp. caraway seeds and shortening. Add rye flour and 2 cups white flour to liquid mixture. Add 1/4 cup white flour as needed. Knead 8 minutes or until dough is no longer sticky. Place in greased bowl, cover and let rise 1 1/2 hours or until doubled in size. Punch down and shape into two 14-inch long loaves. Lightly grease 2 large loaf pans.

continued

Pumpernickel *continued*

Sprinkle pans with corn meal. Place loaves in pans. Make 3 or 4 slashes in top of each loaf, brush with egg white and sprinkle with caraway seeds. Let rise uncovered until doubled. Bake at 350° for 30 - 35 minutes. Cool on racks.

Raisin Bread — Rosinenbrot

2 pkgs. dry yeast
1 tsp. sugar
1/2 cup lukewarm water
8 cups flour, divided
2 tsp. salt
2 Tbsp. butter
1 cup cooked and puréed potatoes
2 cups warm milk
1 egg, slightly beaten
1/2 cup sugar
1/4 cup butter, melted
1 tsp. cinnamon

Filling:
4 Tbsp. butter
1 1/2 cups raisins
1 1/2 cups chopped, candied cherries
1 cup finely chopped nuts
1/2 cup sugar
2 tsp. cinnamon

continued

Raisin Bread *continued*

Dissolve yeast and sugar in lukewarm water. Set aside. Combine 4 cups flour, salt, butter and potato in large mixing bowl. Stir in milk and yeast mixture. Mix thoroughly. Cover and let rise 2 hours or until double in volume. Add egg, sugar, butter and cinnamon. Gradually add remaining flour until dough is no longer sticky. Knead 8-10 minutes. Cover and let rise 1 hour.

To prepare filling: Melt butter. Combine raisins, candied cherries and nuts in a small bowl. Combine sugar and cinnamon separately.

Punch dough down after rising. Divide into 4 parts. Roll each into a 12 x9-inch rectangle. Brush with melted butter, sprinkle with sugar and cinnamon and spread with fruit and nut mixture. Roll rectangle up like a jellyroll, pinching edges together. Place in greased loaf pans, cover and let rise for 1 hour. Preheat oven to 350° and bake for 45 minutes. Remove from pans and brush with melted butter.

Onion Sheetbread — Zwiebelkuchen

1 lb. flour
1 pkg. dry yeast
1/2 cup warm milk
4 Tbsp. melted butter
2 eggs
1 tsp. salt

Spread:
1 3/4 lbs. onions, peeled and sliced
3/4 lb. bacon, diced
4 eggs
1/2 cup sour cream
salt, pepper and paprika
2 Tbsp. caraway seeds

Combine flour, yeast, milk, butter, 2 eggs and salt in a large mixing bowl. Cover and let rise until doubled in size. Fry bacon and onion until onion is transparent. Roll dough out onto greased jellyroll pan. Spread onion and bacon mixture on dough evenly, cover and let rise until dough is just under rim of pan. Whisk eggs, sour cream, salt and spices together and pour over dough. Preheat oven to 325° and bake 20 minutes or until nicely browned. Serve hot with a green salad and dry white wine.

Hard Rolls — Brötchen

1 pkg. dry yeast
1 1/4 cups lukewarm water, divided
2 tsp. sugar
1/2 tsp. salt
2 Tbsp. shortening
1 egg white, stiffly beaten
4 cups flour

Dissolve yeast in 1/4 cup water and set aside. In mixing bowl combine yeast, 1 cup water, sugar, salt and shortening. Fold in stiffly beaten egg white. Add enough flour to make a soft dough. Let dough rise twice until doubled, punch down and let rise again. Punch down and divide into 10-12 pieces. Form into slightly flattened balls and place on a greased baking sheet. Preheat oven to 450° and bake for 20 minutes. To ensure hard crust, place pan with boiling water in bottom of oven during baking.

Pretzels

1 pkg. dry yeast
1 cup lukewarm water
3 cups flour, divided
1 1/2 Tbsp. butter
1/2 tsp. salt
1/2 tsp. sugar
4 cups water
5 Tbsp. baking soda
Coarse salt

Dissolve yeast in lukewarm water. Add 1 1/2 cups flour and the butter, salt and sugar. Beat 4 minutes. Knead in remaining flour until dough is no longer sticky. Cover and let rise . Punch down and divide into 10 pieces. Roll into 20-inch lengths and loop each into twisted pretzel shape. Place on greased baking sheet and let rise until doubled in size. Preheat oven to 475°. Bring 4 cups water and soda to a boil. Using a slotted spoon carefully lower pretzels into water. When they rise to the top return them to greased baking sheet. Sprinkle with coarse salt. Bake about 10 minutes until browned.

Zwieback

7 - 8 cups flour, divided
1/3 cup sugar
2 tsp. salt
1 pkg. dry yeast
2 cups warm milk
1/2 cup shortening
2 eggs, slightly beaten

Mix 3 cups flour, sugar, salt and yeast in large mixing bowl. Combine milk and shortening separately and gradually add to dry ingredients. Beat 2 minutes at medium speed. Add eggs and 1 cup flour to make a thick batter. Beat at high speed for 4 minutes. Add remaining 3 - 4 cups flour. Knead 10 minutes and let rise until doubled. Punch down and let rise again. Shape dough into 6 loaves and place in 9x5-inch loaf pans. Place pans in cold oven, heat to 400°. Reduce heat to 375° after 15 minutes. Continue baking for 25 minutes. Remove bread from pans at once, cool and slice. Place slices on ungreased cookie sheet and bake at 250° until crisp and golden brown.

Fried Mush

3 heaping cups corn meal
2 1/2 cups water
1 1/2 tsp. salt
4 qts. water
1 heaping cup flour

Combine corn meal and 2 1/2 cups water in a large saucepan. Add salt and 4 quarts of water. Cook for 20 minutes. Add flour and mix thoroughly. Pour into a 10x10x3-inch pan. Refrigerate overnight. Slice mush about 1/4 inch thick and deep-fry the slices 4 minutes or until crisp. Serve with honey or maple syrup.

The Kalona Heritage: Amish and Mennonite Culture (Iowa)

Fried Potato Bread

Pickert

1 lb. potatoes
1 pkg. dry yeast
5 Tbsp. warm milk
1 Tbsp. sugar
1 tsp. salt
4 cups flour
5 eggs, separated
2 Tbsp. butter

Peel and grate potatoes. Pour off excess liquid. Combine yeast and warm milk, stir in sugar and set aside. Combine potatoes and salt in a mixing bowl. Gradually stir in flour and egg yolks. Add yeast mixture. Beat egg whites until stiff and fold into potato mixture. Cover and let rise until doubled. Punch down and place in a greased loaf pan. Allow to rise again. Bake at 325° for 1 hour. Remove from pan. When cool, cut bread into 1-inch-thick slices and fry in melted butter until golden.

Salt and bread make cheeks red.

Salz und Brot macht die Backen rot.

Main Course Dishes

A fish should swim thrice: in water, in butter, and in wine.

Der Fisch will dreimal schwimmen: im Wasser, im Schmalz und im Wein.

Sauerbraten

5 lbs. beef rump roast (top or bottom)
salt
3 cups white vinegar
1 large onion, peeled and sliced
2 bay leaves
6 cloves
8 peppercorns
1 Tbsp. pickling spices
1 large carrot, peeled and sliced
4 slices bacon
2 Tbsp. butter
2 large onions, diced
1 additional bay leaf
2 Tbsp. butter
3 Tbsp. flour

Tie beef with string in several places to hold its shape. Rub entire beef with salt and place in deep, close-fitting glass or earthenware bowl. In saucepan combine vinegar, 1 onion, 2 bay leaves, cloves, peppercorns, pickling spices and carrot. Bring to a boil and simmer 5 minutes. Cool and pour over beef.

continued

Sauerbraten *continued*

Meat should be entirely covered by marinade. (If not, add equal parts of vinegar and water to cover.) Cover and refrigerate 3 - 6 days. Turn at least once daily. Remove meat from marinade. Strain marinade and reserve. Dry meat well. (It will not brown properly if wet.) Dice bacon and fry slowly in butter in 5-qt. Dutch oven or casserole. When fat is hot, add meat. Brown quickly on all sides in uncovered pan. Remove meat and add diced onion to brown, stirring frequently to avoid burning. Return meat to pot. Add marinade until it reaches halfway up sides of meat. Add bay leaf. Bring marinade to a boil, cover pot tightly, reduce heat and simmer very slowly but steadily for 3 1/2 - 4 hours, turning 2 or 3 times during cooking. Add more marinade to pot if necessary. (If meat tastes too strong, dilute marinade with water during cooking.) Meat is done when pierced easily with long fork or skewer. Serve with Swabian noodles and a green salad.

Colony Market Place, South Amana, Iowa

Swabian Noodles — Spätzle

4 cups flour	1 egg
1/2 tsp. salt	water

Fill large kettle half-full of water and bring to a boil. Combine flour, salt and eggs in a medium-sized mixing bowl, stirring with a fork. Add water until batter stretches 6-7 inches before tearing when pulled up on spoon. Place large spoonful of batter on wooden cutting board, tilt it over kettle and slice thin strips of batter off into the boiling water. Dip knife into cold water between slices to prevent batter from sticking. Cook for 1 - 2 minutes and remove with a slotted spoon. Drain and place in warmed serving bowl. Continue until batter is gone.

From the New Ulm, Minnesota Cookbook:
"Gemütlicher leben Schwaben und fein, mit schwäbischer Küche und schwäbischem Wein"
(Most happy are the Swabians with their Swabian cookery and Swabian wine)

Stuffed Cabbage Rolls — Kohlrouladen

2/3 cup uncooked rice
1 good-sized head white cabbage
2 lbs. ground beef
1 lb. pork sausage
1 tsp. ground cloves
2 tsp. cinnamon
salt to taste

Cook rice. Cut the core out of the cabbage. Start cooking cabbage with top of head up, then switch the top down so the thickest part gets more steaming. Cook until leaves are pliable and can be removed from head without breaking. Remove cabbage to a large platter. Pull leaves apart carefully and cool. Mix cooked rice, ground beef, sausage and spices together. Form into thick cylindrical patties. Roll in 2 cabbage leaves placed on top of each other. Place rolls in a small, flat roaster.

continued

Stuffed Cabbage Rolls *continued*

Add some water to the pan and cover. Bake at 350° for an hour or more, until tops of rolls are brown and meats are cooked. Check occasionally during baking and baste if leaves are drying. Serve on platter with pan juices. Cabbage rolls reheat well and may also be frozen.

Tongue in Raisin Sauce

Ochsenzunge

1 fresh beef tongue, about 2 lbs.
6 sprigs parsley
1 bay leaf
4 peppercorns
4 whole cloves
1 tsp. salt
1 onion, chopped

2 Tbsp. butter
2 Tbsp. flour
3 Tbsp. tomato paste
1 1/2 cups raisins
2 Tbsp. vinegar
1 tsp. sugar
salt and pepper

Scrub, then soak tongue in cold water for 10 minutes. Place in pot with herbs, spices and onion. Cover with boiling water and simmer uncovered for 1 1/2 hours.

continued

Tongue in Raisin Sauce *continued*

Remove tongue, plunge into cold water, skin and slice. Drain. Reserve stock. Melt butter in a saucepan. Add flour, stirring until brown. Add tomato paste and thin the sauce with reserved stock. Add raisins, vinegar and sugar. Season to taste. Reheat sliced tongue and serve with warm raisin sauce and mashed potatoes.

Westphalian Pepper-Pot

2 cups water
3 onions, chopped
salt to taste
1 tsp. peppercorns
6 whole cloves
2 bay leaves
1 3/4 lb. stewing beef
2 Tbsp. bacon grease
2 Tbsp. flour
2 Tbsp. vinegar
1 tsp. salt

Bring water to a boil in a large pot. Add onions, spices and meat. Simmer until tender, about 2 hours. Remove meat from pot and cut into medium-sized pieces. Strain stock and add water to make 2 cups. Melt bacon grease and add flour, stirring until browned. Stir stock in gradually and season to taste with vinegar and salt. Add meat. Serve with boiled or baked potatoes.

Round Steak Casserole

1 Tbsp. flour
1 slab round steak, cut 1/2 inch thick
salt and pepper
1 Tbsp. butter
2 onions, sliced in rings
1 cup dry white wine

Rub flour, salt and pepper into both sides of steak. Melt butter in a frying pan and brown steak on both sides. Remove from skillet and cut meat into bite-sized pieces. In an ovenproof casserole alternately layer meat and onions. Pour wine over the top. Cover and bake at 350° for 1 1/2 hours.

Beef Stew

Gulasch

2 Tbsp. oil
3 large onions, sliced
1 clove garlic, crushed
3 lbs. stewing beef,
 cut into 1-inch cubes
2 cups hot water
salt and pepper
2 tsp. cornstarch
1 Tbsp. water

Heat oil in large stewing pot or heavy frying pan. Add onions and garlic. Sauté until tender. Add beef and brown on all sides. Pour in water and season with salt and pepper. Reduce heat, cover and simmer until meat is tender, about 1 1/2 - 2 hours. Mix cornstarch and water. Gradually add to stew, stirring until thickened. Serve with boiled potatoes or noodles and a tomato, cucumber or lettuce salad.

Smoked Pork Loin Roast

3 1/2 lbs. smoked pork loin roast
1 cup hot water
1 onion, peeled and quartered
2 tsp. cornstarch
1 Tbsp. cold water
4-5 Tbsp. sour cream

Score surface of meat in criss-cross pattern with sharp knife. Preheat oven to 400°. Place meat fat side up on rack of roasting pan and place in middle of oven. When drippings begin to accumulate, add hot water to avoid burning. Add onion after meat has been in oven 1 hour. Continue baking for 30 minutes. Remove meat from oven and cover to keep warm while making gravy. Place roasting pan on stovetop. Stir well, scraping residue from bottom. Mix cornstarch and water and add to meat juice, stirring constantly. Add sour cream and, if necessary, water until desired consistency is reached. Serve with boiled potatoes and mixed peas and carrots.

Breaded Veal Cutlet — Wiener Schnitzel

4 slices veal cutlet
salt and pepper
1/2 cup butter
1 Tbsp. flour
1 egg, slightly beaten
1/2 cup bread crumbs

Pound cutlets until very thin. Season with salt and pepper to taste. Melt butter in frying pan over low heat. Dip cutlets first in flour, then in egg and finally in bread crumbs. Sauté 2 minutes on each side until brown. Serve with lemon slices, rolled anchovies and capers.

Stuffed Beef Rolls — Rouladen

8 slices round steak, 6x4x1/8-inch (about 3 lbs.)
salt and pepper
1/2 cup flour

Filling:
2 Tbsp. butter
1 1/2 cups finely chopped onion
4 slices bacon, halved
2 Tbsp. salad oil
2 Tbsp. butter
12 small white onions, peeled
2 10 3/4-oz. cans condensed beef broth, undiluted
2 cups finely chopped parsley
2 Tbsp. capers
1 1/2 cups dry red wine, divided
1/2 cup sherry
2 bay leaves, crumbled
8 small carrots, peeled and halved lengthwise

continued

Stuffed Beef Rolls *continued*

Wipe beef with damp paper towels. Sprinkle lightly with salt and pepper. Mix flour with 1 tsp. salt and 1/4 tsp. pepper on a sheet of waxed paper.

To make filling: sauté onion in 2 Tbsp. butter in small skillet. Remove from heat. Add parsley and capers. Mix well.

Place half a slice of bacon and 1/4 cup filling on wide end of each slice of beef. Fold beef over 1/4 inch on narrow sides. Roll up from wide end. Tie with twine. Roll in seasoned flour. Reserve leftover flour. Heat oil and butter in a 6-qt. Dutch oven. Brown beef rolls, a few at a time. Remove from pot when browned.

continued

Stuffed Beef Rolls *continued*

Add whole onions to Dutch oven. Brown. Remove. Return beef rolls to Dutch oven, add undiluted beef broth, 1 cup red wine, sherry and bay leaves. Bring to a boil, reduce heat and simmer, covered, for 1 hour. Add onions and carrots and continue to simmer for another 30 minutes or until tender.

Lift out beef rolls with a slotted spoon. Place on a tray and remove the twine. Mix reserved seasoned flour and 1/2 cup red wine in small bowl. Stir into liquid in Dutch oven. Bring to a boil, reduce heat and simmer, stirring until thickened. Pour over beef rolls and serve with boiled potatoes and a fresh vegetable.

The Amana Barn Restaurant, Amana, Iowa

Braised Rabbit — Hasenbraten

1 rabbit
2 eggs, well-beaten
1 cup flour
2 Tbsp. oil
1/2 - 3/4 cup water
1/2 cup vinegar
1/2 bay leaf
3 peppercorns
1/4 cup chopped onion
2 tsp. cornstarch
salt and pepper

Cut rabbit into serving pieces. First dip pieces in beaten eggs, then in flour. Heat oil in a heavy pan or kettle and fry rabbit on all sides until nicely browned. Add water and vinegar, bay leaf, peppercorns and onion. Simmer for several hours. When meat is tender, remove rabbit and add cornstarch to pan juices to thicken gravy. Season to taste. Serve with dumplings and red cabbage.

Venison Terrine — Wildpastete

1 1/2 lbs. roast venison, diced
1/2 lb. raw venison, minced
1/2 lb. roast pork, diced
2/3 lb. bacon, minced
1 cup Madeira wine
10 small onions, finely chopped
1 Tbsp. butter
1/4 cup finely chopped mushrooms
salt and pepper
1 tsp. thyme
4 slices bacon

Combine meats in a large bowl. Add Madeira. In skillet melt butter and brown the onions. Add to meat along with mushrooms and spices. Grease and flour a 9x5-inch loaf pan. Press meat mixture in firmly. Lay bacon slices on top. Cover tightly with foil and set loaf pan up to about half its depth in a larger pan of boiling water. Bake at 300° for 70 minutes. Remove foil and pour off excess fat. Reverse pan to turn terrine onto serving tray. Slice and serve.

Wild Duck

Wildente

4 wild ducks
1/2 tsp. thyme
2 bay leaves
3 sprigs fresh parsley
dry Concord grape wine
vegetable oil or shortening
salt and pepper
16 small onions
6 Tbsp. butter, divided
1/2 cup dry rhubarb wine
2 cups sliced mushrooms

Singe end feathers of well-cleaned ducks over a flame. Then place birds in a glass, porcelain or stainless steel bowl. Tie herbs up in a cheesecloth and put in bowl. Cover birds with Concord grape wine. Allow to marinate in a cool place or refrigerator at least 24 hours or up to 3 days.

continued

Wild Duck *continued*

When ready to cook, remove ducks, drain and pat exteriors dry with paper towels. Reserve marinade. In large casserole or roaster, sauté ducks in hot oil or shortening, turning to sear all sides. Add strained marinade and bring to a boil.

Sprinkle with salt and pepper. Cover and lower heat to maintain a slow simmer for 1 - 1 1/2 hours. Cooking time depends upon size and age of ducks.

Sauté small onions in 3 Tbsp. butter, turning to soften, but do not allow to brown. Add rhubarb wine and gently poach onions until tender. Do not overcook. Sauté mushrooms in remaining butter for 5 minutes. Add onions and mushrooms to ducks just before serving. (If desired, drippings may be thickened with 1 1/2 tsp. cornstarch blended with 1/4 cup cold water to make gravy.) Serve with boiled potatoes.

Nuremberg Sausage Nürnberger Bratwurst

20 small Nuremberg sausages
1 can beer

Sauce:
3 Tbsp. freshly grated horseradish
1 tsp. salt
3 Tbsp. light cream, whipped
2 tsp. lemon juice
1 tsp. sugar

Sauerkraut:
1 3/4 lbs. drained sauerkraut
1/2 cup water
2 Tbsp. bacon grease
1 Tbsp. sugar
1 onion, sliced
salt and pepper
1 raw potato, grated
2 - 3 juniper berries
1 bay leaf

continued

Nuremberg Sausage *continued*

Brush sausages with beer and fry or grill. Mix horseradish, whipped cream, sugar, salt and lemon juice. Chill. Melt bacon grease in heavy pot. Add onion and sauerkraut, stirring until lightly browned. Add potato, bay leaf, water, sugar and spices. Simmer about 45 minutes, until done. Serve the sausages, sauerkraut and horseradish sauce with thick slices of rye bread.

Bratwurst in Beer Sauce

10 bratwurst
flour
1 Tbsp. butter
1 small can tomato paste
1/2 cup catsup
1 cup tomato juice
1 can beer
1/2 green pepper, diced
1 clove fresh garlic, finely chopped
dash of Worcestershire sauce

Place bratwurst in large pot of hot water for 8-10 minutes. Water must not be allowed to boil! Remove bratwurst, dry with paper towels and roll in flour until covered. Melt butter in frying pan and fry bratwurst until nicely browned.Combine remaining ingredients in saucepan and heat to simmering stage. After bratwurst have been browned, place them in the prepared warm sauce until served. Serve with fried potatoes or French fries and a green salad.

Colony Market Place, South Amana, Iowa

Sauerkraut Casserole

1 lb. ground beef
3/4 cup uncooked rice
1 lb. drained sauerkraut
1 pint chunked tomatoes

Shape enough 1 1/2-inch balls of ground beef to cover bottom of a casserole. Roll each in uncooked rice and place in casserole. Put half of sauerkraut on top of meatballs, then half of the tomatoes. Form flat patties with remaining ground beef and dip only bottom side in rice. Place in casserole. Then layer the remaining sauerkraut and tomatoes. Cover casserole and bake at 350° for 1 1/2 hours.

Beef Noodle Casserole

1 lb. lean ground beef
2 Tbsp. butter
garlic powder to taste
1 tsp. salt
1 tsp. sugar
dash pepper
2 8-oz. cans tomato sauce
1 7-oz. pkg. flat noodles
6 green onions with tops, chopped
1 8-oz. pkg. cream cheese
1 cup sour cream
1/2 cup grated sharp Cheddar cheese

Cook beef in butter until browned and crumbly. Add garlic, salt, sugar, pepper and tomato sauce. Simmer over low heat for 15-20 minutes. Cook noodles and drain. Combine onions, cream cheese and sour cream. After meat sauce and noodles have cooled, grease a 2-qt. casserole. Alternate layers of noodles, cheese mixture and meat sauce in casserole. Repeat. Sprinkle top with grated cheese. Bake at 350° for 15-30 minutes or until cheese is bubbly.

Brick Haus Restaurant, Amana Iowa

Sour Tripe — Saure Kutteln

2 lbs. tripe, blanched and parboiled
2 Tbsp. bacon grease
2 onions, sliced
1 Tbsp. flour
1 cup stock or bouillon
1 bay leaf
1 tsp. chopped lemon peel
3 whole cloves
4 peppercorns
1 tsp. salt
2 tsp. sugar
2 Tbsp. vinegar

Wash tripe and boil for 2 1/2 hours in salted water until tender. Cool and cut into thin slices. Melt bacon grease. Add onions and brown. Sprinkle onions with flour and stir in stock. Add spices and vinegar and cook until liquid is reduced to half. Add tripe and simmer for 30 minutes. Serve with potato dumplings or Swabian noodles.

Sautéed Kidneys — Nieren

1 lb. kidneys
2 Tbsp. butter
1 onion, finely chopped
1 - 1 1/2 cups boiling water
salt and pepper
2 Tbsp. vinegar
1/2 tsp. sugar

Slit kidneys and remove the core. Wash and scald kidneys with hot water. Dry thoroughly. Cut into bite-sized pieces and brown in butter with chopped onion. Add boiling water, salt and pepper. Braise 10-15 minutes and season to taste with vinegar, salt and sugar. Serve with rice.

Pickled Herring Rolls — Rollmops

4 - 6 herring fillets
2 Tbsp. prepared mustard
1 Tbsp. capers
2 small pickles, sliced
2 onions, finely sliced
6 - 8 peppercorns
2 small bay leaves
1 1/2 cups white vinegar
1 cup water, boiled and cooled

Brush one side of each herring fillet with mustard and cover it with capers, pickles and onions. Roll up carefully and secure with cocktail sticks or toothpicks. Place rollmops, peppercorns and bay leaves in a jar. Cover with vinegar and water. Chill for 6 - 8 days. Remove rollmops and serve with boiled potatoes.

Herring in Sour Cream
Matjes nach Hausfrauenart

- 4 - 6 herring fillets
- 1 cup sour cream
- 1/2 cup plain yogurt
- 1 small onion, finely chopped
- 1 small apple, diced
- salt and pepper
- vinegar to taste

Cut herring into bite-sized pieces. Combine sour cream, yogurt, onion and apple. Add herring. Season with salt, pepper and vinegar to taste. Refrigerate for several hours. Serve with boiled potatoes.

Vegetables

Laurels won't fill your stomach; you're better off with potatoes.

Lorbeer macht nicht satt, besser wer Kartoffel hat.

Baby Peas and Carrots

Erbsen und Karotten

1 lb. small carrots
2 Tbsp. butter
1/2 cup water
1 8-oz. can baby peas, drained
1 tsp. salt
1 tsp. sugar
1 Tbsp. chopped parsley

Peel carrots. If they are small, leave them whole; if not, cut into 3-inch strips. Melt butter in a saucepan and add carrots, stirring until they are coated. Add water and cook 10-15 minutes, until tender. Add peas and heat. Season with salt and sugar. Sprinkle with parsley and serve.

Red Cabbage — Rotkohl

1 small head red cabbage
3 Tbsp. bacon grease
2 medium-sized apples, diced
1 cup water
4 Tbsp. vinegar
4 Tbsp. sugar
1/2 tsp. salt
1/4 tsp. pepper
1/2 tsp. ground cloves

Remove coarse outer leaves from cabbage. Cut head into four pieces, remove the hard core and shred finely. Melt bacon grease in a large pot, add cabbage and apple, stirring until well-mixed. Add water, vinegar and spices. Cook until tender, about 1 hour. Stir frequently. Serve with pork or game.

In Bavaria this dish is called "Blaukraut" or blue cabbage, since it is cooked until it turns a light shade of purple.

Curly Kale   Grünkohl

4 lbs. fresh curly kale or
4 10-oz. pkgs. frozen chopped kale
2 Tbsp. bacon grease
1 large onion, chopped
3 Tbsp. prepared mustard
2 Tbsp. quick oats
6 smoked sausages

Trim fresh kale, removing thick stalks and ribs. Slice in thin strips. Heat grease in a large heavy pot. Add onion and stir until transparent. Add kale and enough water to cover bottom of pot. Mix thoroughly. Cover and cook over low heat until tender, about 45 minutes. Stir in mustard and oats and lay sausages on top of kale. Replace lid and continue to simmer for 20 minutes. Serve with boiled potatoes.

Black Forest Asparagus

2 -3 lbs. fresh asparagus
1 tsp. salt
2 tsps. sugar
2 1/2 cups flour
2 eggs
1/2 tsp. salt
milk as needed
1/2 lb. smoked ham, sliced
4 Tbsp. melted butter

Trim asparagus, cutting off woody ends. Cook asparagus upright in a steamer with 1/2 cup boiling water or in a flat pan cover asparagus with boiling water. Add salt and sugar to cooking water. Cook 12-20 minutes, depending on size and tenderness. Remove and drain. Combine flour, eggs, salt and enough milk to make a thin pancake batter. Fry pancakes in a hot skillet and reserve. When asparagus is tender, remove from pot and wrap 1-2 stalks in a pancake. Place rolled pancakes on a platter with the sliced ham. Before serving, pour melted butter over pancakes.

Deep-Fried Asparagus   Spargel in Backteig

1 1/2 cup flour
2 tsps. salt, divided
1 tsp. oil
1/2 cup beer
2 eggs, separated
2 1/2 lbs. fresh asparagus
1 Tbsp. sugar
fat for frying

In a mixing bowl combine flour, 1 tsp. salt, oil and beer. Add egg yolks to batter. Cover and let stand for 1 hour in a warm place. Wash and trim asparagus. Cook in boiling water with 1 tsp. salt and 1 Tbsp. sugar for 12 - 20 minutes or until tender. Remove and drain. Just before using, beat egg whites until stiff and fold into batter. Dip asparagus stalks into batter and fry in hot fat until crisp and brown.

Sautéed Cucumbers — Schmorgurken

2 cucumbers
3 Tbsp. butter
1 tsp. salt
1 Tbsp. sugar
1 tsp. pepper
1 1/2 Tbsp. vinegar
2 tsps. flour
1 cup finely chopped dill

Pare, seed and dice cucumbers. Melt butter in a skillet. Add cucumber, salt, sugar, pepper and vinegar and cook over medium heat for about 20 minutes. Sprinkle in flour, stirring to thicken. Add dill right before serving. Serve with smoked pork and boiled potatoes.

Cauliflower in White Sauce — Blumenkohl

1 medium-sized cauliflower
3 Tbsp. butter
3 Tbsp. flour
1 tsp. ground nutmeg
1 Tbsp. lemon juice
1 tsp. salt
1 egg yolk

Remove leaves from cauliflower and trim, removing blemishes and stem. Soak in cold, salted water for about 15 minutes. Place cauliflower head-up in a pot of boiling water. Cover and cook until tender, 15-20 minutes. Remove and reserve 2 cups of cooking water for white sauce. Melt butter in a saucepan, add flour and stir until browned. Gradually add reserved warm cooking water, stirring constantly. Simmer for 10 minutes. Season with nutmeg, lemon juice and salt. Stir in egg yolk just before serving. Pour sauce over cauliflower and serve.

Deep-Fried Vegetables   Gemüse in Backteig

1 lb. vegetables (carrots, cauliflower, brussel sprouts, kohlrabi, celery, broccoli and tomatoes)
1/2 cup flour
1 egg
1 tsp. salt
1/2 cup milk
1 tsp. oil
fat for frying

Wash and cut or break vegetables into bite-sized pieces. Steam vegetables until almost tender. Combine flour, egg, salt, milk and oil to make a smooth batter. Dip vegetables into batter with a fork. Lower coated vegetables into hot fat carefully and fry until brown and crisp. Remove and drain on paper towels. Serve with mayonnaise and cold-cuts.

Vegetable Croquettes — Gemüsekroketten

1 lb. vegetables (cabbage, kohlrabi
or celeriac)
1 onion, finely chopped
1 Tbsp. butter
1 - 2 eggs
1/4 cup fine bread crumbs
1/2 tsp. salt
1 Tbsp. finely chopped fresh herbs
3 Tbsp. bread crumbs
fat for deep-frying

Clean vegetables, steam and chop finely or mince. Sauté the onion in butter and add to vegetables along with eggs and 1/4 cup bread crumbs. Season with salt and fresh herbs. Roll stiff mixture into cylinders, coat with bread crumbs and fry until golden brown. Drain on paper towels.

Puréed Peas — Erbsenpüree

1 1/2 cups dried peas
2 1/2 cups water
1 carrot
1 stalk celery
1 onion
1 tsp. salt
3 Tbsp. butter
1/4 cup diced bacon
1 onion, sliced

Soak peas in water for 12-24 hours. Bring to a boil in same water and cook for 1 1/2 hours. Add whole carrot, celery and onion and continue cooking for 30 minutes. Remove carrot, celery and onion from pot and purée peas. Return peas to pot, add salt and butter and reheat. Fry bacon and sliced onion. Place peas in serving bowl, garnish with onion and bacon mixture and serve. Good with pork roast and sauerkraut.

Caraway Potatoes — Backofenkartoffeln

2 1/4 lbs. small new potatoes
2 Tbsp. caraway seeds
1 tsp. salt
2 Tbsp. melted butter

Scrub, but do not peel potatoes. Cut them in half. Combine caraway seeds and salt in a saucer. Dip cut edge of potatoes into caraway and salt mixture and place cut edge down on a greased baking sheet. Brush with melted butter and bake at 325° for 30-40 minutes or until tender.

Sautéed Potatoes — Butterkartoffeln

2 1/4 lbs. small new potatoes
4 Tbsp. butter
1 tsp. salt
sugar

Scrub potatoes but do not peel. Boil until tender, about 20 minutes. Remove from pot, rinse with cold water and peel immediately. Melt butter in frying pan. Add peeled potatoes and salt. Turn potatoes frequently to ensure even browning. Sprinkle with a trace of sugar when done. Serve with bratwurst or curly kale.

Boiled Potatoes — Geschmeltzte Kartoffeln

1 1/2 lbs. potatoes
2 Tbsp. butter
1/2 cup bread crumbs

Scrub, peel and quarter potatoes. Boil until tender. Fry crumbs in butter until golden brown. Drain potatoes when done and return pot to hot burner for about a minute to let excess moisture steam off. Place potatoes in serving bowl. Pour crumbs over top and serve.

Potatoes, Curds and Oil
Pellkartoffeln, Quark und Leinöl

2 1/2 lbs. potatoes
1 lb. large curd cottage cheese
2 Tbsp. chives
4 Tbsp. vegetable oil

Scrub potatoes, but do not peel. Boil until tender, about 20 minutes. Combine cottage cheese and chives in a serving bowl. Remove potatoes from pan, rinse under cold water and peel immediately. Place in a separate serving bowl. Pour oil over potatoes and serve with cottage cheese.

# Potato Ring		Kartoffelring

1 1/2 lbs. potatoes
1/4 cup butter
3 eggs, separated
1 tsp. salt
1 tsp. ground nutmeg

Scrub and peel potatoes. Boil until tender. Drain. Rub through a sieve or purée while still hot. Set aside to cool. Cream butter in a mixing bowl. Gradually blend in egg yolks. Stir in the cooled potatoes, salt and nutmeg. Beat egg whites until stiff and fold into the potato mixture. Put into a well-greased tube pan and bake at 325° for 30-40 minutes. Reverse pan onto serving tray to remove ring. Center of ring may be filled with stew or steamed vegetables.

Potato Croquettes — Kroketten

1 1/2 lbs. potatoes
2 Tbsp. butter
2 eggs, divided
1 cup flour
1 tsp. salt
1 tsp. ground nutmeg
1/2 cup bread crumbs
fat for deep-frying

Scrub and peel potatoes. Boil until tender. Drain and purée immediately. Cool. Cream butter in a mixing bowl. Gradually add 1 egg, potatoes, flour, salt and nutmeg. Shape the stiff mixture into cylinders about 2 inches long, dip into one slightly beaten egg and coat with bread crumbs. Deep-fat fry at once until golden brown. Serve with a roast and vegetable.

Potato Pancakes — Kartoffelpuffer

2 1/4 lbs. potatoes
1 egg
1 onion, grated
2 Tbsp. flour
1 tsp. salt
2 Tbsp. oil

Peel and finely grate the raw potatoes. Drain off any liquid in potatoes after grating. Add egg, onion, flour and salt. If mixture seems too moist, add more flour. Heat oil in a skillet. Drop 3 or 4 spoonfuls of potato mixture into skillet at a time, pressing each down firmly with a spatula to form a pancake. Fry on both sides until golden brown. Serve immediately with applesauce and cinnamon.

In southern Germany, potato pancakes are known as "Reibekuchen".

Potato Dumplings — Semmelknödel

4 cups boiled, riced potatoes
1/2 cup flour
1/2 tsp. salt
1/4 tsp. pepper
4 slices white bread, cubed

1 large onion, finely chopped
3 Tbsp. butter
2 eggs
1/3 cup minced parsley
2 Tbsp. butter
3/4 cup dry white bread crumbs

Combine riced potatoes, flour, salt and pepper. Brown cubed bread and onion in butter until onions are transparent. Add to potato mixture along with eggs and parsley. Mix and shape into golf ball-sized dumplings. Place in pot of boiling water or stock. Do not crowd. Cook 5-7 minutes until dumplings float to top. Drain and keep warm. Fry bread crumbs in butter until crisp. Spoon over dumplings before serving.

Bill Zuber's Restaurant, Homestead, Iowa, Amana Colonies

Thuringian Dumplings Rohe Kartoffelklösse

3 lbs. potatoes
1 cup milk
1 tsp. salt
1/4 cup butter
1 1/3 cups semolina flour
1/2 cup bread crumbs

Peel and grate potatoes into a bowl of water. Wrap them in cheesecloth and squeeze out as much liquid as possible. In a saucepan bring milk, salt and butter to a boil. Add semolina, stirring constantly until a solid mass has formed. Continue cooking for about 1 minute, then remove from heat and stir in dry potatoes. Dust hands with flour and shape mixture into 3-inch dumplings. Coat each dumpling with bread crumbs and drop into salted, boiling water. Simmer until dumplings float to top, about 12-15 minutes. Serve with sauerbraten, game or any roast.

Five fingers hold more than two forks.

Fünf Finger fassen mehr als zwei Gabeln.

Cakes and Desserts

The oldest trees often bear the sweetest fruit.

Die ältesten Båume tragen oft die süssesten Früchte.

Berlin Doughnuts — Berliner Pfannkuchen

1 pkg. dry yeast
5 cups flour
1 cup sugar
1 1/4 cups milk, divided
1/3 cup butter, melted
2 eggs
1 tsp. salt
apricot or plum jam
fat for deep-frying
powdered sugar

Dissolve yeast in 1/4 cup warm milk. Combine flour, yeast, sugar, milk, melted butter, eggs and salt in a large mixing bowl. Beat at medium speed for 4 minutes. Cover and let rise until double in size. Roll dough out to 1/4-inch thickness. Cut out round circles with a glass or a cookie cutter. Place 1 tsp. jam on every other round and cover it with another round, pinching edges together. Allow to rise again. Deep-fat fry doughnuts until golden brown. Remove and place on paper towels to drain. Dust with powdered sugar when cool.

Bavarian Sweet Rolls — Rohrnudeln

1 pkg. dry yeast
5 Tbsp. sugar, divided
1/2 cup warm milk
5 cups flour
2 eggs
1 jigger rum
1/2 cup butter, melted

Dissolve yeast and 1 Tbsp. sugar in warm milk and set aside. Blend flour, 4 Tbsp. sugar, eggs, rum and yeast mixture in a mixing bowl and beat for 3 minutes. Cover and let rise until doubled. Punch dough down. Dip a tablespoon in melted butter; scoop up spoonfuls of dough and arrange them in close rows in a greased glass baking dish. Brush top and sides of each roll with melted butter as you go along. Bake at 325° for 30 minutes. Serve hot. Good with vanilla sauce or stewed plums.

German French Toast — Arme Ritter

5 hard rolls
2 egg yolks
1 Tbsp. sugar
1 tsp. salt
1 cup milk
2 eggs, slightly beaten
5 Tbsp. bread crumbs
2 Tbsp. butter
cinnamon and sugar

Cut rolls in half and place them on a plate. Combine egg yolks, sugar, salt and milk and pour over buns evenly. Allow rolls to soak until liquid is absorbed. They should not become soggy and break! Dip buns in beaten eggs and coat with bread crumbs. Fry in hot butter on both sides until golden brown. Sprinkle with cinnamon and sugar and serve hot.

Oma's Apple Dumplings — Apfelklösse

3 Tbsp. cold butter
4 cups flour, sifted
1 egg, beaten
1 cup sour cream
1 tsp. salt
1 Tbsp. sugar
1 tsp. flour
1 tsp. baking soda
1 Tbsp. water
20 apples, peeled and cored
sugar
cinnamon
butter
1/4 cup boiling water

Cut butter into flour. Mix egg, sour cream, salt and sugar. Add 1 tsp. flour. Dissolve soda in 1 Tbsp. water and mix ingredients together. Handling very lightly and as little as possible, roll dough into 2 sheets as for pie crust. Cut into 6 to 7-inch squares.

continued

Oma's Apple Dumplings *continued*

Make about 20 squares in all. Put one apple on top of each square. Sprinkle sugar, dash of cinnamon and dab of butter over each apple. Fold corners of squares over apple, pinch to secure, and place in a greased baking dish. Sprinkle with more sugar and cinnamon, and dab with butter. Place 1/4 cup boiling water in bottom of dish and bake at 375° until apples are soft and dumplings are golden brown. Serve with sweet cream.

Bill Zuber's Restaurant, Homestead, Iowa, Amana Colonies

Funnel Cakes — Drechter Kucha

3 eggs
1 qt. milk
3 tsp. baking powder
flour
vegetable oil
powdered sugar

Combine eggs, milk and baking powder in a mixing bowl. Add enough flour so that batter will run through a funnel. If it is too thick and will not flow well, add more milk. If it runs through too fast, add more flour. Pour enough oil in a frying pan to cover the bottom and heat. The temperature of the oil is critical for successful frying. Dip a fork into batter and then hold it in hot oil. If it sizzles, the oil is hot enough. Pour thin stream of batter into oil in a spiral motion, beginning in middle and moving out. Fry cake until brown on one side, then flip it over and brown the other side. Remove and sprinkle with powdered sugar. Best when eaten immediately.

Pennsylvania Dutch Folk Culture Society, Lenhartsville, Pennsylvannia

Westphalian Bread Pudding

6 slices dry pumpernickel
1 cup hot milk
4 eggs, separated
4 Tbsp. sugar
2 oz. chocolate, grated
1 tsp. cinnamon
1 jigger rum
3 Tbsp. lemon juice
1/2 cup chopped nuts
1/3 cup raisins

Crumble pumpernickel into a mixing bowl. Pour hot milk over pumpernickel and let stand for 1 hour. Add remaining ingredients except for egg whites and mix thoroughly. Beat egg whites until stiff and fold into pudding mixture. Grease and flour a large baking dish and fill it with pudding mixture. Cover and set in a larger pan of boiling water in oven. Bake at 350° for 1 hour. Reverse dish onto serving plate to remove pudding and serve with applesauce or hot vanilla or chocolate sauce.

Apples in a Blanket

Äpfel im Schlafrock

2 1/2 cups flour
1/3 cup sugar
1/2 cup butter
1 tsp. salt
1/2 tsp. baking powder

4 tart apples
1 jigger rum
sugar
4 Tbsp. currant or raspberry jam
2 egg yolks, slightly beaten

Combine flour, sugar, butter, salt and baking powder in a mixing bowl, to make dough. Chill. Peel and core apples. Pour some rum and sugar into core cavity of each apple and set aside for 2 hours. Roll out dough and cut into 4 squares large enough to wrap around apples. Place apple in center of each square. Spoon 1 Tbsp. jam in core cavity of each apple. Pull corners of dough up and around apple, covering it completely. Brush with egg yolk and bake in a greased baking dish at 350° for 30 minutes. Serve with warm Vanilla Sauce.

Vanilla Sauce — Vanillesauce

1 1/2 cups milk
2 tsp. vanilla extract
2 Tbsp. sugar
2 egg yolks
1/2 tsp. cornstarch

Heat milk and vanilla in top of double boiler. Set aside to cool. Blend sugar, egg yolks and cornstarch until smooth. Add to milk, stirring until thoroughly blended. Return to stove and cook in double boiler over moderate heat, stirring constantly until thickened. Serve hot or cold with puddings, yeast breads or over fresh fruit.

Plum Cake — Zwetschkenkuchen

3 3/4 cups flour
1 tsp. baking powder
2 eggs
1 3/4 cups sugar, divided
3/4 cup butter
3 1/2 lbs. fresh damson plums

Sift flour and baking powder onto a large board or clean countertop. Make a hollow in the middle. Crack eggs into hollow, add 3/4 cup sugar and stir. Scatter dots of butter over flour and knead all ingredients together until dough is smooth and soft. Refrigerate for 30 minutes. Wash and pit plums, slitting them in half so that they lay flat, yet are still connected. Roll dough out onto greased jellyroll pan. Cover dough with overlapping rows of plums. Sprinkle with 1/2 cup sugar and bake at 350° for 30 minutes. Remove from oven and sprinkle with remaining 1/2 cup sugar. Serve with whipped cream.

Blackberry Cake — Brombeerkuchen

3 cups flour
2 cups sugar
1 tsp. salt
1 tsp. ground nutmeg
1 tsp. cinnamon
1 tsp. ground cloves
3 eggs, beaten

1 cup butter, melted
1 cup buttermilk
1 1/2 cups fresh blackberries
1 Tbsp. baking soda
1/2 cup chopped pecans or walnuts
1/2 cup raisins

Combine flour, sugar, salt, nutmeg, cinnamon and cloves in a large mixing bowl. Add eggs, butter, buttermilk and blackberries. Beat for 1 minute at medium speed. Stir in soda, pecans and raisins. Spoon batter into a greased and floured 10-inch tube pan. Bake at 350° for 55-60 minutes, or until cake tests done.

Brick Haus Restaurant, Amana, Iowa

Moravian Sugar Cake

2 cakes yeast
1 cup lukewarm water
1 cup hot mashed potatoes
1 cup sugar
1 cup butter, melted
2 eggs
1 Tbsp. salt
flour
butter
1 lb. brown sugar
cinnamon

About 7 p.m. dissolve yeast in lukewarm water and let sit for 5 minutes. In large mixing bowl combine mashed potatoes, yeast mixture, sugar, melted butter, eggs, salt and enough flour to make a stiff dough. Dough should pull off spoon, leaving it almost clean. Cover and let rise overnight. Next morning put in 8x8-inch pans, spreading dough to about 3/4 inch thick. Let rise again, about 1 1/2 hours, or until puffy. With thumb, make rows of holes about 2 inches apart. Fill holes with butter and some brown sugar. Sprinkle cake with cinnamon. Bake at 400° for 15-20 minutes.

Fruit Cake — Obstkuchen

1 cup milk
1 1/2 cups sugar, divided
1 Tbsp. salt
1 cake compressed yeast
1 cup lukewarm water
6 cups sifted flour
6 Tbsp. shortening, melted

3 Tbsp. butter, melted
2 cups sliced apples, rhubarb, pitted cherries or sliced peaches
2 Tbsp. flour
1 egg, beaten
2 Tbsp. cream

Scald milk, 1/2 cup sugar and salt together. Cool until lukewarm. Dissolve yeast in lukewarm water and add to cooled milk. Add 3 cups of flour and beat until smooth. Add melted shortening and remaining flour. Knead well. Place in a greased bowl, cover and let rise until double in bulk, about 3 hours.

continued

Fruit Cake *continued*

This makes enough dough for five 9-inch cakes. Store extra dough in refrigerator. Roll out 1/5 of quantity and place in a greased 9-inch pie plate; make a high rim of dough around outside. Brush with butter and sprinkle with 1/4 cup sugar. Let rise. Press prepared fruit close together into dough. Sprinkle remaining 3/4 cup of sugar and flour over fruit. Before baking combine beaten egg and cream and spoon over fruit. Cover cake with a pan and bake for 10 minutes at 425°, then remove pan from top and continue baking at same temperature for another 25 minutes.

Bill Zuber's Restaurant, Homestead, Iowa, Amana Colonies

Rhubarb Cream Pie — Rhabarberkuchen

1 unbaked 9-inch pie shell
rhubarb, sliced
1/2 cup cream
1/2 cup water
2 eggs, separated
1 cup sugar
2 Tbsp. flour

Put rhubarb in pie shell. Mix cream, water, egg yolks, sugar and flour. Pour over rhubarb. Bake at 375° until custard-like. Beat egg whites to a stiff peak, slowly adding sugar while beating and spread on top of pie. Return to oven until brown on top. This pie cannot be frozen or reheated.

The Kalona Heritage: Amish and Mennonite Culture (Iowa)

Frankfurt Tube Cake

Frankfurter Kranz

Cake:
2/3 cup butter
3/4 cup sugar
5 eggs
1 1/4 cups flour
3/4 cup corn meal
1 tsp. baking powder
2 Tbsp. rum
1 Tbsp. lemon juice

Filling:
1 1/8 cups butter
2 cups powdered sugar
3 egg yolks
1 tsp. vanilla extract

Topping:
2 tsp. butter
1/2 cup chopped almonds
2 Tbsp. sugar

continued

Frankfurt Tube Cake *continued*

For cake: Cream butter in large mixing bowl. Add sugar and eggs. Beat until light. Stir in flour, corn meal, baking powder, rum and lemon juice until well-blended. Grease and flour a 10-inch tube pan. Pour in batter and bake at 350° for 45 minutes. Cool slightly before removing from pan.

For filling: Cream butter and blend in remaining ingredients until creamy.

For topping: In butter and sugar brown almonds until golden.

To assemble: Slice cake in half cross-wise. Spread filling on bottom layer and cover with top layer. Ice top and sides of cake with filling and sprinkle with topping.

Black Forest Cherry Cake
Schwarzwälder Kirschtorte

Cake:

10 eggs, separated
1 cup sugar
2 tsp. vanilla extract
2 Tbsp. rum
2/3 cup unsweetened cocoa
1 1/2 cups flour

Fillings:

1 large can cherry pie filling
5 Tbsp. kirschwasser
1 qt. light whipping cream
3 Tbsp. powdered sugar
1 tsp. vanilla extract
10 - 15 maraschino cherries
2 oz. chocolate, grated

continued

Black Forest Cherry Cake *continued*

For cake: Beat egg whites in large mixing bowl until stiff. Gradually add sugar, vanilla and rum. Beat egg yolks in one at a time. Sift flour and cocoa together and gradually fold into batter. Pour into 2 greased 10-inch springforms or 4 greased 9-inch round cake pans. Preheat oven to 400° and bake for 15 - 25 minutes or until cake tests done. Cool 5 minutes before removing from pans. Cut cakes into 2 layers horizontally if springforms are used.

For fillings: Stir cherry-pie filling and kirschwasser together. Whip cream in a large mixing bowl, adding powdered sugar and vanilla just before stiff peaks form.

To assemble: Place 1 cake layer on cake tray. Spread with 1/2-inch layer of whipped cream mixture. Top with second cake layer. Spread with all of cherry-pie filling. Top with third cake layer and again spread with whipped cream mixture. Place final layer on cake and spread remaining whipped cream on top and sides. Decorate cake with maraschino cherries and grated chocolate. Do not make cake too far in advance, as whipped cream does not hold its shape very long.

Raisin Pie

1 cup raisins
1 1/2 cups sugar
1/4 cup flour
1 tsp. salt
2 cups water
1 egg, beaten
2 Tbsp. grated lemon peel
3 Tbsp. lemon juice
1 unbaked pie shell and strips of dough for lattice work

Rinse raisins and set aside. Mix sugar, flour and salt in top of double boiler. Stir in water gradually. Add raisins. Bring to a boil, stirring constantly and cook for 1 minute. Remove from heat. Stir small amount of this hot mixture into egg and then add egg to mixture in double boiler. Cook over simmering water for 5 minutes. Remove from heat and stir in lemon peel and juice. Cool. Pour into pie shell and cover with lattice strips. Bake at 450° for 10 minutes. Reduce heat to 350° and continue baking for 30 minutes.

Black Walnut Pie

1/2 cup butter
1 cup firmly packed dark brown sugar
1 cup dark corn syrup
4 eggs, slightly beaten
1/2 tsp. salt
1 tsp. vanilla extract
1 unbaked pie shell
1 cup black walnut meats

Cream butter and brown sugar in mixing bowl. Stir in corn syrup, eggs, salt and vanilla. Pour mixture into pie shell. Arrange walnuts symmetrically on top and bake at 375° for 40-45 minutes until set.

Brick Haus Restaurant, Amana, Iowa

Grandma's Coffee Cake — Oma's Kuchen

2 1/2 cups milk, divided
1 cake compressed yeast
1 Tbsp. sugar
5 1/2 - 6 cups flour
1/2 cup shortening
1 cup sugar
1 cup raisins
1 1/2 tsp. salt
1 egg, beaten
sugar and cinnamon

Scald 1 1/2 cups milk. When cool, stir in yeast and 1 Tbsp. sugar until dissolved. Add 1 1/2 cups flour to make a soft sponge. Put in warm place until it bubbles, about an hour. When sponge is ready, melt the shortening. Add remaining milk, sugar, raisins. salt and egg to melted shortening. Mix all of it into sponge. Add 4-4 1/2 cups flour to make dough stiff enough to handle. Cover and let rise until light. Form into 2 loaves and place in 9x5-inch loaf pans. Brush tops with melted butter and sprinkle with sugar and cinnamon. Let rise. Bake at 375° for 25-30 minutes.

Old-Fashioned Fruit Cake — Obstbrot

2 eggs
1 lb. mild pork sausage
2 cups sugar
3 cups flour
1 tsp. baking soda
1 cup hot water

1 lb. dates, pitted and diced
1 cup chopped nuts
1 jar candied fruit, finely chopped
1 tsp. cinnamon
1 tsp. allspice
1/4 tsp. cloves

Combine eggs, sausage, sugar and flour in a mixing bowl. Dissolve soda in hot water and add to sausage mixture. Add remaining ingredients and mix thoroughly. Place dough in greased loaf pan and bake at 350° for 1 hour.

Apple Streusel Pie

Apfelkuchen

3 cups sliced apples
1 9-inch unbaked pie shell
1/2 tsp. cinnamon
4 Tbsp. butter, divided
2/3 cup sugar
2 eggs
1 tsp. salt
1 1/2 tsp. vanilla extract
3 oz. cream cheese, softened
1/3 cup brown sugar
1/2 cup flour
1/2 cup chopped pecans

Place apples in pie shell and sprinkle with cinnamon. Cream 2 Tbsp. butter, sugar and eggs. Add salt, vanilla and cream cheese. Blend until just smooth and pour over apples. Combine brown sugar, flour, 2 Tbsp. butter and pecans. Crumble this mixture on top of pie. Bake at 375° for 45 minutes. Reduce heat to 350° and continue to bake for 15 minutes. *Historic Strasburg Inn, Strasburg, Pennsylvania*

Shoofly Pie

1 unbaked 9-inch pie shell
1 cup molasses
1/3 cup hot water
1/2 tsp. cinnamon
1/4 cup butter
1/2 cup brown sugar
1/2 tsp. baking soda
1 cup flour

Mix molasses and hot water. Pour into pie shell. Combine remaining ingredients in a separate bowl and crumble over top of pie. Bake at 375° for 15 minutes. Reduce heat to 350° and bake for 45 minutes.

This is a favorite item with visitors at the Historic Strasburg Inn, Strasburg, Pennsylvania, *and has been popular with natives of the Pennsylvania Dutch country for years. It is both delicious and inexpensive to make, thus satisfying 2 basic needs of the Pennsylvania Germans —the love of good cooking and the desire for frugality.*

Nut Pudding — Nusscreme

1 1/2 Tbsp. or 6 sheets gelatin
1/2 cup water, divided
1/2 cup sugar
1 tsp. vanilla extract
2 tsp. rum
1 pint heavy cream
1 cup ground nuts

Soak gelatin in 1/4 cup cold water in saucepan. Add remaining 1/4 cup water, sugar, vanilla and rum and stir over low heat until dissolved. Refrigerate for 20 minutes. Whip cream until really stiff. Carefully fold in nuts. Then fold whipped cream mixture into gelatin. Refrigerate until set. Garnish with whole nuts and additional whipped cream.

Red Fruit Pudding — Rote Grütze

2 lbs. red fruit (raspberries, currants, cherries, strawberries, rhubarb)
2 cups water
1 cup red wine
2 Tbsp. honey
1 Tbsp. lemon juice
1/4 cup port wine or sherry
1/4 cup cornstarch

Use any combination of fruits listed above. Wash fruit, pit cherries and cut rhubarb into inch-long pieces. Place fruit in a saucepan. Stir in water, wine, honey and lemon juice. Cook over low heat until fruit is tender. Mix port or sherry and cornstarch. Add to fruit mixture, stirring constantly until thickened and clear. Pour into serving dishes and chill. Serve with whipped cream or vanilla sauce.

Bavarian Cream

Bayerische Creme

1 1/2 cups whipping cream, divided
1 Tbsp. unflavored gelatin
2 eggs, separated
1/4 cup sugar
1/2 tsp. vanilla extract

Combine 1/2 cup cream and gelatin in a saucepan. Let stand 5 minutes. Add additional 1/2 cup cream and stir over low heat until gelatin dissolves. In separate bowl combine egg yolks, sugar and vanilla. Stir in gelatin mixture and refrigerate until set, about 15 minutes. Beat egg whites untill stiff. In separate bowl whip remaining 1/2 cup cream. Fold stiff egg whites and then whipped cream into gelatin mixture. Pour into serving dish or mold and refrigerate for 3-4 hours. Garnish with fruit and whipped cream.

Rice Pudding — Reisauflauf

1/2 cup uncooked rice
1 1/2 cups milk
1/4 cup sugar
2 Tbsp. butter
4 eggs, separated

Combine rice, milk and sugar in top of double boiler. Cook until rice is done and all milk has been absorbed. Cool to room temperature. Cream egg yolks and butter. Add to cooled rice. Beat egg whites until stiff and fold into rice until just blended. Pour into a greased 1 1/2-qt. baking dish and bake at 300° for 1 hour. Serve with fruit or as is.

The Christmas Room, Amana, Iowa

Raspberry Snow

Himbeerschnee

1 qt. fresh raspberries
1/2 cup sugar
2 Tbsp. white wine
2 egg whites

Reserve 8-10 raspberries for garnish. Purée remaining raspberries or rub through a sieve. Add sugar and wine, stirring well. Beat egg whites until stiff and fold into raspberry mixture. Pour into serving dish and freeze until firm. Garnish with whole raspberries and serve with whipped cream.

Elisabeth's Strawberries   Erdbeeren Elisabeth

1 qt. strawberries
1/2 cup sugar
2 Tbsp. cognac or brandy
1 Tbsp. unflavored gelatin
1 cup cold water
1 cup whipping cream

Reserve 8-10 strawberries for garnish. Purée remaining strawberries and mix with sugar and cognac or brandy. Soften gelatin in cold water and place over hot water to dissolve. Stir into strawberry mixture. Whip cream until stiff and fold into purée. Pour into serving dish or mold. Chill. Decorate with strawberries and serve with additional whipped cream.

Pfeffernüsse

2 eggs
2 cups packed brown sugar
1 tsp. baking soda
1 Tbsp. hot water
2 cups flour
1/2 tsp. cinnamon
1/4 tsp. mace
1/4 tsp. salt
1 cup chopped nuts
powdered sugar

Beat eggs lightly, then add brown sugar, one tablespoon at a time. Continue to beat. Dissolve soda in hot water and stir into egg-sugar mixture. Sift flour, spices and salt together. Stir into batter and then add nuts. Chill and shape into small balls. Place balls on lightly greased baking sheet. Bake at 375° for 6 - 8 minutes until lightly brown. Remove from oven and roll in powdered sugar.

Hermann Cookbook, Hermann, Missouri

Grandma's Christmas Yeast Cake
Oma's Weihnachtsstollen

4 pkgs. dry yeast
1 cup lukewarm water
5 lbs. flour
1 Tbsp. salt
2 1/2 lbs. sugar
1 tsp. nutmeg
2 tsp. cinnamon

3/4 lb. melted butter
1/2 cup candied citron, diced
1 1/2 qts. warm milk
1/2 lb. raisins
1/2 tsp. almond extract
2 cups nuts, coarsely cut
(almonds, pecans and English walnuts in combination)

Dissolve yeast in lukewarm water. Add 2 cups flour and mix well. Cover and let rise until double in bulk. Sift remaining flour into large pan together with salt, sugar, nutmeg and cinnamon. Add yeast mixture, melted butter, citron and milk.

continued

Grandma's Christmas Yeast Cake *continued*

Knead 10 minutes. Add raisins, almonds extract and nuts. Knead again until well-blended. Let rise again until doubled. Divide dough into 8 parts. Shape each to fit a greased loaf pan. Cover and let rise again until double in bulk. Just before baking, cut a deep gash down center of each loaf. Bake at 350° for 50 minutes. When done brush well with melted butter and sprinkle with powdered sugar and cinnamon.

Hunger is the best cook.

Hunger ist der beste Koch.

Notes

Notes

Notes

Notes

Notes

H.E.B.